My Aunt Came
Back from
Louisiane

My Aunt Came Back from Louisiane

Traditional Song Adapted
and Illustrated by Johnette Downing

PELICAN PUBLISHING COMPANY
GRETNA **2008**

The word "Pelican" and the depiction of a pelican
are trademarks of Pelican Publishing Company, Inc.,
and are registered in the U.S. Patent and Trademark Office.

Library of Congress Cataloging-in-Publication Data

Downing, Johnette.
   My aunt came back from Louisiane : traditional song / adapted and illustrated by Johnette Downing.
       p. cm.
   Summary: In this variation on the traditional song, the narrator's aunt makes repeated trips to Louisiana, returning with a bag of red beans from New Orleans, gumbo from Thibodaux, peaches from Ruston, and so on. Includes sheet music plus facts about the places mentioned in the song.
   ISBN 978-1-58980-607-8 (hardcover : alk. paper) 1. Folk songs, English--United States--Texts. [1. Folk songs--United States. 2. Louisiana--Songs and music.] I. Title.
   PZ8.3.D75397My 2008
   782.42--dc22
   [E]

                                                2008009674

Printed in Singapore
Published by Pelican Publishing Company, Inc.
1000 Burmaster Street, Gretna, Louisiana 70053

*In memory of my mother, who always had
a song in her heart and a child on her knee*

My aunt came back from New Orleans
and she brought me back a bag of red beans.

My aunt came back from Thibodaux
and she brought me back filé gumbo.

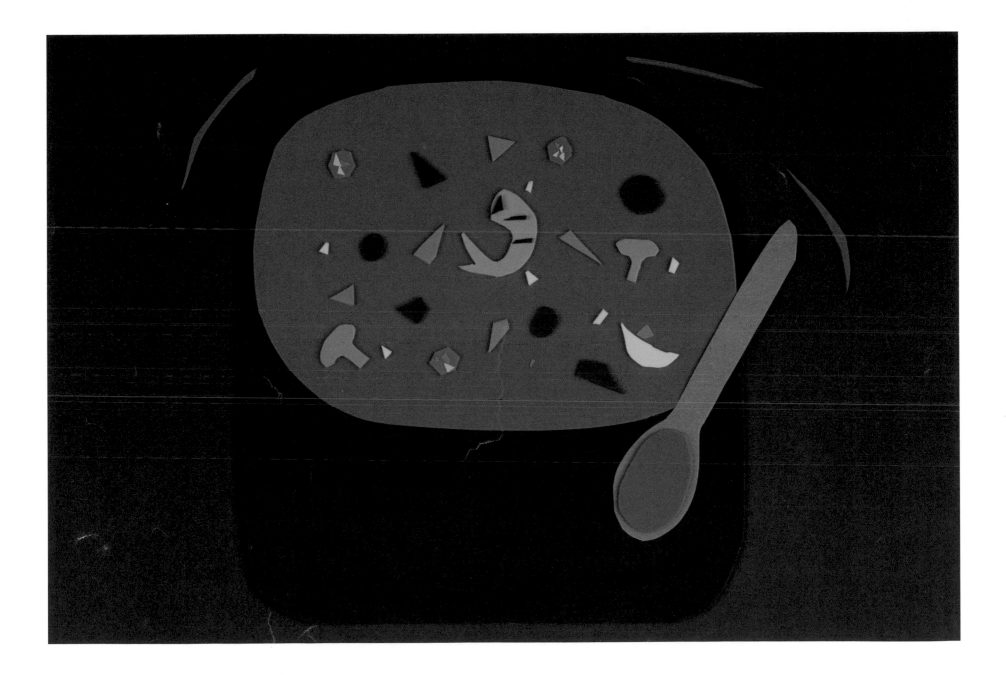

My aunt came back from li'l Chauvin
and she brought me back an accordion.

My aunt came back from Lafayette
and she brought me back a French baguette.

My aunt came back from Evangeline
and she brought me back a violin.

My aunt came back from 'ti Mamou
and she brought me back some crawfish stew.

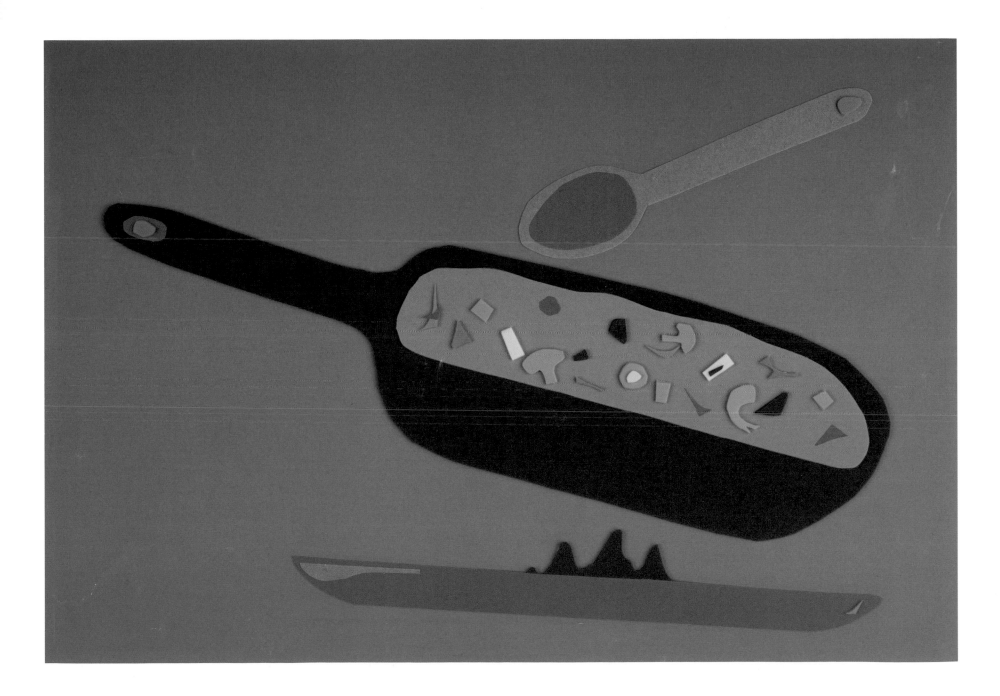

My aunt came back from Natchitoches
and she brought me back a meat-pie dish.

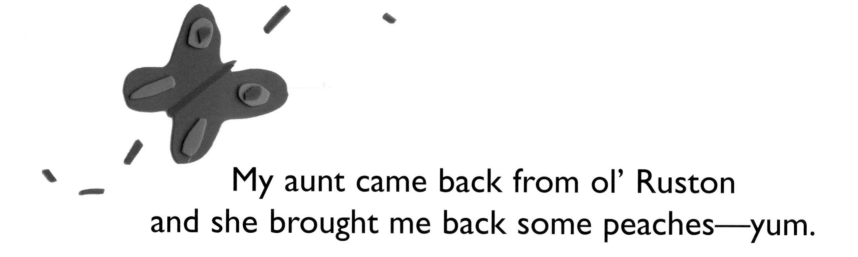

My aunt came back from ol' Ruston
and she brought me back some peaches—yum.

My aunt came back from Franklinton
and she brought me back a watermelon.

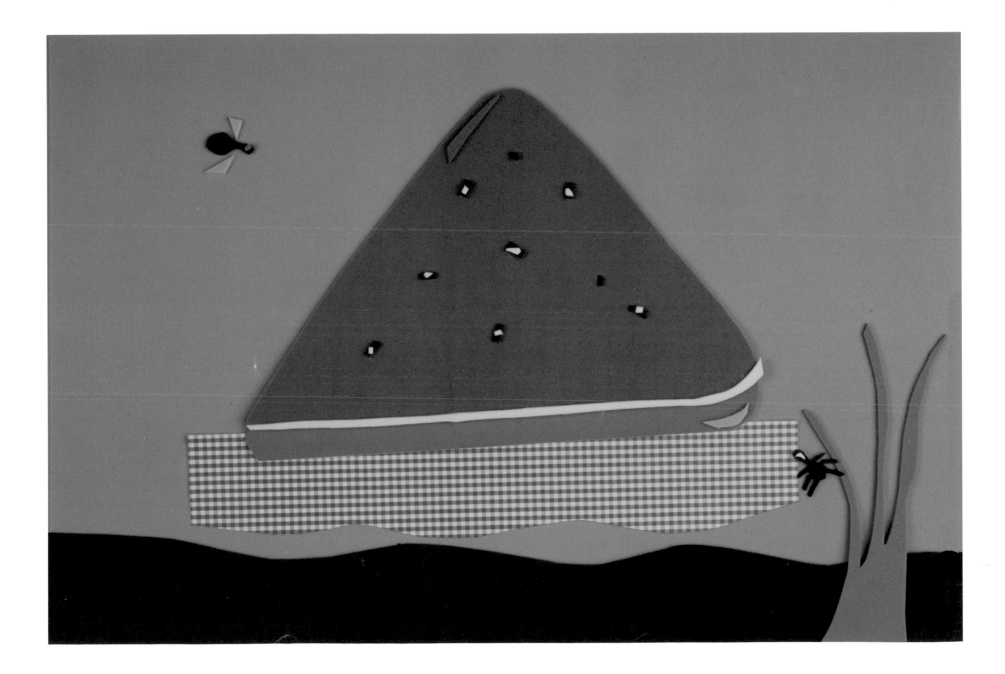

My aunt came back from Albany
and she brought me back a strawberry.

My aunt came back from the Vieux Carré
and she brought me back a sweet beignet.

My aunt came back from Louisiane
and she's going back as soon as she can.

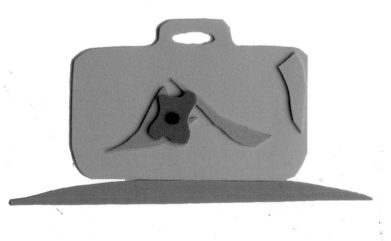

Word Map

Albany is a Hungarian settlement in southeast Louisiana known for its large, sweet strawberries.

Chauvin (Shoh-van) is a Cajun-French bayou town in south Louisiana known for its seafood and music. The Cajun **accordion** came to Louisiana from Germany and is an important part of Cajun music.

Evangeline (Ee-van-juh-lin) is a Cajun-French town in southwest Louisiana known for Cajun music. A **violin,** or fiddle, is an instrument used in traditional Cajun music.

Franklinton is a town in southeast Louisiana known for its sweet watermelons.

Lafayette (Laff-ee-et) is a Cajun-French city in southwest Louisiana known for spicy food, music, and festivals. A **baguette** (bag-et) is a long, dense loaf of bread.

Louisiane is the original French name for Louisiana.

Mamou (Mam-oo) is a Cajun-French town in southwest Louisiana known for spicy food, zydeco music, Cajun music, dance halls, and Cajun Mardi Gras (*Courir de Mardi Gras*). **'Ti** (tee) is short for *petit*, which means "little" in French. **Crawfish stew** is a spicy dish made with the tail meat of crawfish.

Natchitoches (Nack-uh-dish) is a Native American settlement and the original French colony in Louisiana. The historic town in northwest Louisiana is known for its delicious **meat pie,** a semicircular flaky pastry stuffed with seasoned ground beef.

New Orleans, the birthplace of jazz, is a multicultural city on the Mississippi River in southeast Louisiana known for Creole and French food, Mardi Gras, and music. **Red beans** are traditionally served over rice for dinner on Mondays in New Orleans.

Ruston is a town in north Louisiana known for its juicy peaches.

Thibodaux (Tib-a-doh) is a Cajun-French town in south Louisiana known for its spicy food. **Filé** (fee-lay) is dried sassafras leaves crushed into a fine powder. **Gumbo** is a thick soup made with okra and seafood or chicken and sausage.

Vieux Carré (view ka-ray), or French Quarter, is the oldest neighborhood in New Orleans. The French Quarter is famous for **beignets** (ben-yayz), pastries that are deep fried until puffy, then sprinkled generously with powdered sugar.

MY AUNT CAME BACK FROM LOUISIANE

Traditional Song with Adapted Lyrics by Johnette Downing

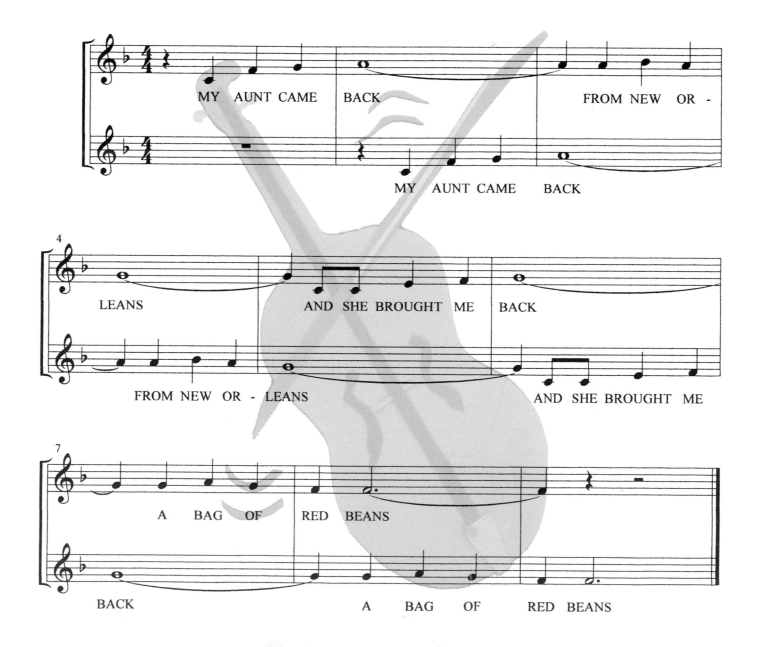